The Mermaid's Guide to
Magical Coping

Amanda Aliff, LPC

Copyright © 2025 by Amanda Aliff, LPC, NCC, CCTP

All rights reserved. No part of this book may be reproduced or transmitted in any form or by any means, electronic or mechanical, including photocopying, recording, or by any information storage and retrieval system, without permission in writing from the copyright owner. This book was printed in the United States of America.

ISBN (Paperback): 978-1-961752-45-0
ISBN (Hardcover): 978-1-961752-46-7
ISBN (Kindle): 978-1-961752-47-4

Available on Amazon and other retail outlets.

To all the mermaids out there—

The ones who ride the waves of life with courage,
who sparkle in their own unique way,
who lift others up like a rising tide,
and who keep swimming, even when the waters get rough.

May you always believe in your magic,
find strength in your journey,
and let your light shine as brightly as the sea under the moon.

This book is for you—because the ocean would not be the
same without your beautiful ripples.

With love and mermaid magic.

Welcome to the Mermaid's Guide to Magical Coping!

Ahoy, young mermaid!

Life under the sea is full of wonders—sparkling treasures, swaying seaweed, and shimmering waves. But even in the most magical of oceans, stormy seas can roll in. Sometimes, we feel tangled like seaweed, lost in the deep, or caught in a riptide of emotions. That is why every mermaid needs a special set of skills to navigate the waves of life!

This book is your ocean map to calm waters. Inside, you will discover A-Z coping skills, each inspired by the magical world of mermaids. From breathing like a bubble to riding the ripples, these skills will help you handle worries, sadness, frustration, and even those moments when you feel like a storm is brewing.

Whether you are swimming through smooth waters or facing a mighty sea creature of stress, you have the power to find your way back to peace. Every mermaid has a unique strength—this book will help you find yours!

So, grab your seashell journal, flip your fins, and let's dive deep into the magic of mindfulness, resilience, and self-care. The ocean is calling, and you are ready!

Let's make waves, one coping skill at a time!

ANCHOR YOUR FEELINGS

Sometimes, big feelings can make you feel like you are floating in a stormy sea—tossing and turning like a little boat in the waves. But do you know what helps boats stay steady? An anchor!

An anchor keeps a boat in place, even when the waves are rough. You can use your own special anchor to help you feel safe and calm when your emotions feel too big.

Try this mermaid trick:

⚓ Take a deep breath—like a mermaid filling her lungs before a big dive.

⚓ Find something to hold onto—hug a pillow, squeeze your hands together, or press your feet into the floor.

⚓ Say to yourself: "I am safe. I am strong. I can handle this."

When you feel like your emotions are carrying you away, drop your anchor by using these steps. The waves will calm, and you will feel steady again—just like a strong, confident mermaid in the sea!

BREATHE LIKE A BUBBLE

Sometimes, when you feel upset, nervous, or angry, your breathing might get fast—just like waves crashing against the rocks!

But mermaids know a special trick to feel calm again.

They breathe like bubbles!

Bubbles float gently through the water, moving slowly and peacefully. When you breathe like a bubble, you can help your body and mind relax too!

Try this mermaid trick:

- ◯ Take a deep breath in through your nose, filling up your belly like a big, round bubble.

- ◯ Blow out slowly through your mouth, like you are sending a bubble gently floating away.

- ◯ Watch it in your mind as it drifts into the sky, taking your worries with it.

- ◯ Repeat a few times until you feel calm and light—just like a bubble floating on the waves!

Next time you feel like a storm is brewing inside, just breathe like a bubble and let your worries drift away.

CREATE A CORAL COVE

Every mermaid needs a special place where they feel safe, cozy, and happy— a Coral Cove! This is your very own magical hideaway, where you can relax and feel peaceful when big feelings come.

Try this mermaid trick:

🪸 Close your eyes and imagine your perfect Coral Cove. Is it a secret shell cave, a warm sandy shore, or a glowing underwater castle? Fill it with things you love—maybe soft seaweed pillows, twinkling treasure chests, or friendly sea creatures.

🪸 Pretend to visit your coral cove whenever you need to feel safe.

🪸 Make a real Coral Cove at home— set up a quiet space with pillows, stuffed animals, or a cozy blanket!

Your Coral Cove is always there for you —a safe and happy place to swim back to anytime you need a break.

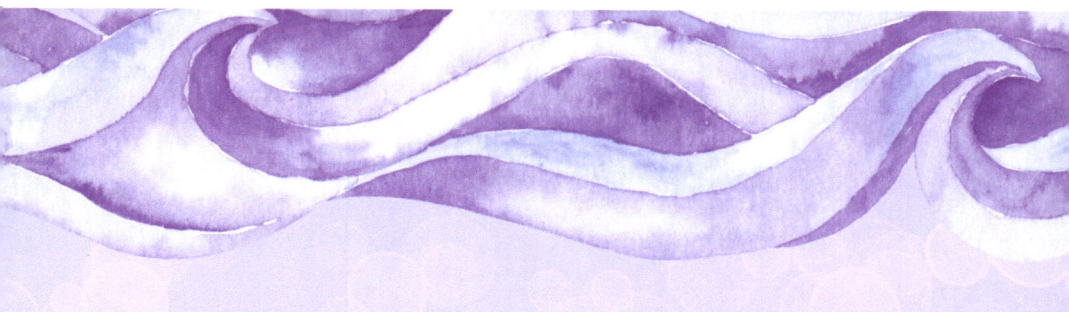

Mermaids love telling exciting stories about their underwater adventures! But did you know that writing down your own thoughts and feelings can help you feel better and braver?

Journaling is like letting your feelings flow onto paper, just like ocean waves rolling onto the shore.

Try this mermaid trick:

- Draw a picture of how you feel—if you are happy, maybe it is a sunny beach; if you are sad, maybe it is a rainy sea.

- Write a little note about your day—what made you smile? What was tricky?

- Pretend your journal is a message in a bottle—write down your feelings and imagine sending them off to sea.

Remember: There is no right or wrong way to journal—just let your feelings swim free!

Your journal is a safe place for your thoughts, just like a treasure chest full of your most important feelings!

ECHO POSITIVE THOUGHTS

Did you know that dolphins send sounds through the ocean to talk to each other? You can do the same with kind words to yourself! When you say something positive, it echoes back and helps you feel stronger and happier.

Try this mermaid trick:

- Think of a happy thought, like "I am brave!" or "I am a great friend!"

- Say it out loud, like a dolphin sending a message across the sea.

- Repeat it again and again, letting your voice bounce back like an echo!

- Feel the words fill you up, making your heart feel warm and bright!

The more you repeat your happy thoughts, the stronger they become—just like a mermaid's magical song floating through the sea!

FLIP YOUR FINS

When mermaids feel stressed, they do not sit still—they SWIM! Moving your body helps shake off worries and makes you feel happier and lighter.

Try this mermaid trick:

- Pretend to be a mermaid—wiggle your arms like seaweed or kick your legs like fins!

- Jump like a dolphin, spin like a seahorse, or wiggle like a jellyfish! Run, dance, stretch, or play outside—anything that makes your body feel happy and free.

- Imagine swimming through the waves, letting all your stress float away behind you!

Next time you feel tense or restless, just flip your fins and swim your worries away!

GATHER SEASHELLS OF GRATITUDE

Mermaids love collecting beautiful seashells, just like you can collect happy thoughts! Even on stormy days, there is always something special to find if you look for it.

Try this mermaid trick:

- Think of three things that make you smile—maybe a hug, your favorite snack, or a fun game. Imagine putting those thoughts into a treasure chest in your heart.

- Draw or write about them in a special journal.

- Whenever you feel sad, open your heart's treasure chest and remember all the good things inside!

The more seashells you gather, the happier your heart feels —just like a mermaid finding hidden treasures!

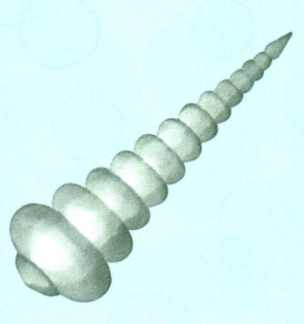  

HUM A SIREN SOUND

Mermaids use their songs to calm the sea, and you can calm your heart and mind with music too! Singing, humming, or listening to a tune can help you feel peaceful when you are feeling overwhelmed.

Try this mermaid trick:

- Hum your favorite tune or make up a silly mermaid song.
- Sing softly like a mermaid under the moonlight.
- Listen to calm music and let it wash over you like gentle waves.
- Move with the rhythm, swaying like seaweed in the current

Music carries away worries, just like the ocean carries away little ripples in the water!

IMAGINE AN OCEAN ADVENTURE

When you feel worried or upset, you can take a trip to a magical place in your mind. Mermaids love to explore the deep blue sea—and you can too!

Try this mermaid trick:

🦀 Close your eyes and picture yourself swimming through a sparkling blue ocean.

🦀 Imagine friendly dolphins and glowing fish guiding you.

🦀 Feel the warm sun on your face as you float on the water.

🦀 Take a deep breath and enjoy your adventure!

Your imagination is like a magic portal—it can take you anywhere you want to go!

JELLYFISH JITTERS

Ever feel like you have too much energy, or your body just cannot sit still? That is okay! Mermaids are not made to sit still for too long—they wiggle and move, just like a jellyfish floating in the water.

Try this mermaid trick:

🪼 Shake your arms like jellyfish tentacles.

🪼 Jump up and down like a dolphin splashing.

🪼 Wiggle and dance until your body feels light and happy!

🪼 Take a deep breath and feel the calm waves return.

Moving helps release extra energy, making you feel calm and free, just like a jellyfish drifting peacefully in the sea!

KEEP YOUR
TIDE BALANCED

Mermaids follow the ocean's rhythm, and you can too by having a good routine! Taking care of your body and mind helps you feel happy and strong every day.

Try this mermaid trick:

🌙 Get plenty of sleep, so you feel rested like a mermaid floating in calm waters.

🌙 Eat healthy foods to keep your energy up—think of it as fuel for your fins!

🌙 Make time for play, rest, and learning, just like a mermaid swimming with the tide.

🌙 Listen to your body—when you are tired, rest; when you are hungry, eat; when you are full of energy, move!

Keeping your tide balanced helps you feel your best, so you can keep swimming strong!

LET THE CURRENTS FLOW

The ocean is always moving—sometimes the waves are gentle, and sometimes they are wild and stormy. But no matter what, the current keeps flowing, and the sea always finds its way back to calm waters.

Just like the ocean, your feelings come and go—sometimes you are happy, sometimes you are sad, and sometimes you are unsure. And that is okay! You do not have to fight your feelings—just let them flow, like the ocean waves.

Try this mermaid trick:

🐢 Close your eyes and imagine your feelings as waves in the ocean.

🐢 If you are feeling sad, mad, or worried, picture those feelings rising up like a wave.

🐢 Take a deep breath and as you exhale, let the wave roll back into the sea.

🐢 Remind yourself: Feelings come and go. Just like the ocean, I will find calm again.

You do not have to stop the waves—just let them flow and trust that every wave eventually finds its way back to peace.

MAKE THE MERMAID MOOD BOARD

Mermaids love collecting treasures—beautiful seashells, sparkling pearls, and shiny sea glass. But did you know that you can collect happy thoughts and dreams too? A Mermaid Mood Board is a special place where you can gather all the things that make you feel happy, inspired, and brave!

Try this mermaid trick:

🐙 Find a piece of paper, a notebook, or a small poster board—this will be your mermaid treasure map!

🐙 Cut out pictures, draw, or write things that make you feel happy—maybe a favorite animal, a big dream, or kind words.

🐙 Decorate it with stickers, glitter, or even real seashells to make it shine like an underwater treasure!

🐙 Hang it up where you can see it every day to remind yourself of all the things that bring you joy.

Whenever you need a boost of happiness, look at your mood board and let it fill you with mermaid magic!

NAVIGATE STORMY SEAS

Sometimes, life feels like a big stormy ocean—waves crashing, winds howling, and everything feeling a little out of control. But just like a brave mermaid or sea captain, you can steer your way through the storm and find calm waters again!

Try this mermaid trick:

- Take a deep breath—just like a mermaid diving under the waves.

- Look for a solution—every storm has a way through! Ask yourself, "What can I do to make this better?"

- Break it down into small steps—like following a treasure map one clue at a time.

- Ask for help if you need it—even the best sailors have a crew!

No storm lasts forever, and you are strong enough to navigate any rough waters. Keep going, keep swimming, and soon you'll find calm seas ahead!

OPEN UP LIKE A CLAMSHELL

Sometimes, when we feel sad, mad, or worried, we want to close up tight like a clamshell hiding its pearl. But did you know that talking about your feelings can help you feel lighter and happier? Just like a clamshell opens to reveal something beautiful inside, you can open up and share your feelings too!

Try this mermaid trick:

🐚 Find a trusted person—a parent, teacher, or friend who will listen.

🐚 Take a deep breath and start small—just saying "I am feeling a little sad today" is a great start!

🐚 Use words, drawings, or even a whisper—however you feel comfortable.

🐚 Remember, you do not have to hold everything inside!

When you open up like a clamshell, you let others help and support you—because your feelings are important, and you never have to face the waves alone!

PAINT THE OCEAN BREEZE

When words are hard to find, colors, shapes, and pictures can help your feelings swim free! Just like the ocean paints the sky with sunrise colors, you can use art to express your emotions in a way that feels just right for you.

Try this mermaid trick:

★ Choose colors that match your mood—blue for calm, yellow for happy, red for excitement, or any color that feels right!

★ Paint, draw, or scribble—it does not have to be perfect, just let your hands move like ocean waves.

★ Create a sea scene, a storm, a treasure map, or even a magical mermaid world!

★ Let your feelings flow onto the page, just like the ocean breeze carries waves across the sea.

Art helps release big feelings and turns them into something beautiful—just like the sea turning a tiny grain of sand into a pearl!

QUIET THE WAVES

Sometimes, our minds feel like a stormy ocean—thoughts crashing like big waves, making it hard to feel calm. But just like the sea eventually settles, you can quiet the waves in your mind and find your inner peace.

Try this mermaid trick:

- Sit or lie down in a comfy spot.
- Close your eyes and imagine a calm ocean with gentle waves.
- Take a slow, deep breath in—like the tide rising.
- Breathe out slowly—like the waves gently rolling back to sea.
- Repeat this a few times, feeling the storm inside settle into soft ripples.

Whenever your thoughts feel too loud, just take a moment to quiet the waves—soon, you will feel as peaceful as a mermaid floating in the sea.

RIDE THE RIPPLES

Sometimes, things do not go as planned—maybe a fun day gets canceled, a friend does not want to play, or something feels unfair. It is easy to get frustrated, but mermaids know a secret—instead of fighting the waves, they ride the ripples!

Try this mermaid trick:

- Take a deep breath—imagine you are floating on gentle waves.

- Remind yourself: "I cannot control everything, but I can choose how I react."

- Look for a new way to have fun—if one wave does not work, another one will come!

- Smile and keep swimming—even small ripples can lead to big adventures!

Life does not always go the way we expect, but if you ride the ripples instead of fighting them, you will always find your way to brighter waters!

SHINE LINE A PEARL

Every mermaid starts as a tiny shell in the ocean, just like a pearl begins as a small grain of sand. But over time, that little grain grows and shines into something beautiful and special—just like YOU!

Sometimes, you might feel small or unsure of yourself, but remember—you have your own special sparkle that no one else has. Maybe you're really good at drawing, making people laugh, or being kind to others. Those are your treasures!

Try this mermaid trick:

- Think of one thing that makes you special—maybe it is something you love to do or something that makes you a great friend.

- Say it out loud: "I shine bright like a pearl because I am ___!" (kind, creative, brave, funny, etc.)

- When you feel unsure, imagine yourself as a glowing pearl in the ocean, shimmering with all the wonderful things that make you YOU!

Remember: Even if you do not always see your shine, it is always there—just like a pearl hidden inside a seashell, waiting to sparkle!

TELL A TREASURE TALE

Mermaids love telling exciting stories about their underwater adventures! But did you know that you can create your own treasure-filled tales to help your heart feel lighter?

When you use your imagination to make up a story, you give your feelings a chance to swim free—just like a message in a bottle drifting across the sea!

Try this mermaid trick:

- Start with a "Once upon a tide..." and let your story flow like the ocean.

- Make yourself the hero—maybe you are a brave mermaid, a clever dolphin, or a curious sea explorer!

- Give your story a challenge to solve—a lost treasure, a magical sea creature, or a riddle from a wise old turtle!

- Draw or act out your tale to make it even more fun.

Every story you tell is a little treasure that shows how creative, smart, and special you are! So grab your seashell notebook and let the ocean of your imagination take you on an adventure!

UNDERWATER UNWIND

Even the busiest mermaids need time to rest and relax. When the waves feel wild, and your mind is full of too many thoughts, it is time to slow down and unwind—just like a mermaid floating peacefully beneath the sea.

Try this mermaid trick:

- Find a quiet, comfy spot to sit or lie down.
- Close your eyes and take a slow, deep breath—imagine you are sinking into soft, warm water.
- Let your arms and legs feel weightless, like seaweed swaying in the ocean.
- Breathe in calm and breathe out stress.
- Stay here for a few moments, feeling peaceful, like a mermaid resting in a cozy coral cove.

Relaxing is just as important as playing! Whenever you need a break, take a deep breath and let yourself unwind like a mermaid floating in the sea.

VISUALIZE A MERMAID LAGOON

When life feels a little too busy, and your mind is full of crashing waves, you can close your eyes and escape to a peaceful mermaid lagoon!

A mermaid lagoon is a magical place where the water is calm, the sun sparkles on the waves, and everything feels safe and happy. Just by imagining it, you can help your body relax and feel at peace.

Try this mermaid trick:

- Close your eyes and take a deep breath, like you are about to dive into the water. Picture a secret mermaid lagoon— what does it look like? Is it glowing blue, filled with coral castles, or surrounded by singing dolphins?

- Listen for the sounds—gentle waves, the splash of a tail, or a soft ocean breeze. Feel the warmth of the sun and the cool, smooth water around you.

- Stay in your lagoon for as long as you like, letting all your worries drift away.

When you open your eyes, you will feel refreshed and calm, just like a mermaid floating peacefully in her hidden paradise!

WHISPER TO THE WHALES

Did you know that whales sing gentle songs across the ocean to talk to one another? Just like whales use their voices to send messages of love and comfort, you can use kind words to help yourself feel strong and brave!

Sometimes, we say mean things to ourselves without even realizing it—like "I am not good enough" or "I cannot do this." But just like a whale sings calm and powerful songs, you can whisper kind words to yourself that make you feel better.

Try this mermaid trick:

- Place your hands over your heart and take a deep breath. Whisper a kind message to yourself, like "I am strong," "I am loved," or "I can do hard things."

- Imagine a giant, gentle whale swimming near you, listening to your words and echoing them back.

- Repeat your message a few times, letting it fill you up like a warm ocean current.

The more you whisper kind words to yourself, the more your heart will believe them—just like a whale's song travels far and wide across the sea!

X MARKS THE SPOT

Every great mermaid adventure starts with a treasure map—and guess what? You can make your own! When you set a goal and take small steps toward it, you are on a journey to find your hidden treasure—your success!

Even if the path has twisty turns and wavy waters, if you keep swimming forward, you will get closer and closer to your goal—just like a pirate searching for treasure!

Try this mermaid trick:

- Think of a goal you want to reach—maybe learning a new skill, making a new friend, or finishing a fun project.

- Draw your treasure map! Your goal is the X on the map, and each step is a seashell, rock, or starfish leading the way.

- Take one small step at a time—even tiny splashes move you closer!

- Celebrate every little victory—each step gets you closer to your treasure!

Remember, every mermaid adventurer faces waves along the way, but if you keep swimming, you will always find your treasure!

YEARN FOR THE SUNLIGHT

Just like mermaids swim to the surface to soak up the warm sun, we all need a little sunshine and fresh air to feel our best! Spending time outside can boost your mood, give you energy, and help you feel calm and happy—just like the sun shining down on the sea.

Try this mermaid trick:

☀ Step outside and take a deep breath—feel the fresh air fill your lungs.

☀ Close your eyes and feel the warmth of the sun on your skin, like a mermaid floating near the surface.

☀ Listen to nature—birds singing, the rustling of leaves, or even the sound of the breeze.

☀ Move your body—run, jump, dance, or simply stretch your arms like a starfish!

Even on cloudy days, getting outside can help you feel refreshed and full of mermaid energy! So swim toward the sunlight and let nature fill you with warmth and joy.

ZOOM THROUGH THE WAVES

Mermaids do not stay still for too long—they splash, dive, and zoom through the ocean! When you feel stressed, restless, or full of big emotions, moving your body helps you shake it all off and feel strong and free!

Try this mermaid trick:

⭐ Jump like a dolphin, flipping high above the waves!

⭐ Spin like a seahorse, twirling and twirling until you giggle!

⭐ Wiggle like a jellyfish, letting all the stress drift away.

⭐ Run, dance, stretch, or swim—move in a way that makes you feel happy and light!

Exercise is like an ocean current—it keeps your energy flowing and washes worries away. So next time you need a boost, zoom through the waves and let your body feel the joy of movement!

Magical Mermaid Affirmations

Whenever you feel like the waves are getting rough, take a deep breath and repeat these mermaid affirmations to yourself:

I can handle any storm that comes my way.

I trust my heart to guide me through the waves.

I spread joy like sunlight on the sea.

I am as strong as the ocean currents.

I ride the waves of life with courage.

I am a shimmering pearl of wisdom and kindness.

I let my emotions flow like the tides.

Whenever you need a boost of mermaid magic, come back to these affirmations and say them with confidence!

A Closing Message from the Ocean

Dear Mermaid,

You swam through an ocean of coping skills, learning how to stay afloat in rough waters and ride the waves of your emotions. Remember, every mermaid faces storms, but with patience, courage, and the right skills, you can always find your way back to calm waters.

No matter what challenges you face, you are never alone—your mermaid heart is strong, and your treasure chest of coping skills will always be there to help you shine.

So, keep swimming, keep believing in yourself, and never forget—you are a powerful mermaid, ready to make waves!

With love and ocean magic.

Keep the Magic Flowing!

Loved this book? The Magical Mermaid Mindset Series has even more enchanting adventures waiting for you!

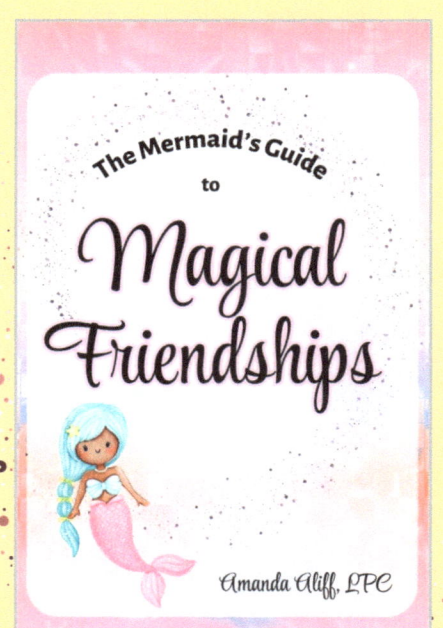

Discover the secrets to making strong, kind, and lasting friendships under the sea! Learn how to communicate, resolve conflicts, and be a true friend.

Shimmer and shine with self-belief! Find the courage to embrace your unique sparkle, face challenges, and swim through life with confidence.

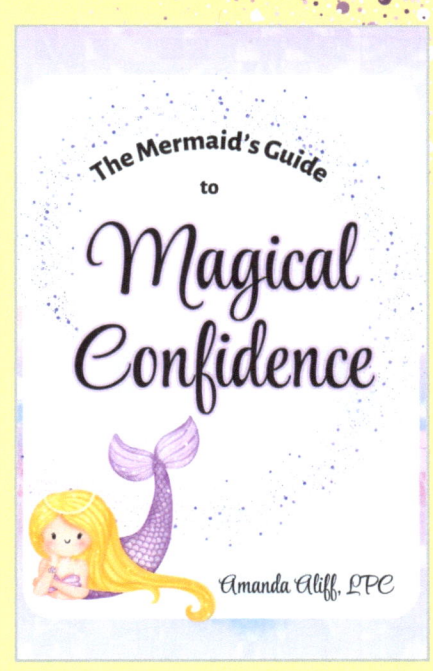

Find them all on Kindle and paperback!

Keep swimming, keep believing, and never forget— your magic is limitless!

www.ingramcontent.com/pod-product-compliance
Lightning Source LLC
Chambersburg PA
CBHW042039050526
44107CB00107B/1038